Original title:
The Northern Echo

Copyright © 2024 Swan Charm
All rights reserved.

Author: Sebastian Sarapuu
ISBN HARDBACK: 978-9916-79-438-8
ISBN PAPERBACK: 978-9916-79-439-5
ISBN EBOOK: 978-9916-79-440-1

Ethereal Dances on Frozen Waters

Whispers glide on icy breath,
Shimmers cast in moonlit depth.
Figures twirl, unseen and free,
Crystals join in harmony.

Echoes sway in tranquil night,
Frozen dreams take silent flight.
Underneath the poised expanse,
Ghostly shadows weave their dance.

Myths Beneath Northern Stars

Legends breathe in frosty air,
Stories wrapped in silver glare.
Constellations guard their tales,
As the night wind softly wails.

Ancient spirits roam the skies,
In the dark, their whispers rise.
Each star a gem, a thought, a wish,
Time suspended in the abyss.

Enchanted Trails Through Frozen Solitude

Footprints trace in fresh white snow,
Paths where only wild dreams go.
Silence reigns, a sacred hush,
Through the woods, a gentle rush.

Echoes dance along the trees,
Laced with whispers of the breeze.
In solitude, the heart can find,
Wonders few have seen, refined.

Glacial Serenade Under Cosmic Veils

Glacial hymns in stillness sing,
Notes escaping winter's wing.
The cosmos weaves its soft embrace,
Melodies of time and space.

Crystalline with ethereal glow,
Rippling tides in starry flow.
Each note a chill, each pause a gleam,
Dreams unfurl like rivers' stream.

Luminaries Among the Frosted Pines

Stars glimmer soft in the night,
Their light dances on snowy white.
Whispers of winds through the trees,
Carry secrets upon the breeze.

Moonlight bathes the frosted ground,
In this peaceful place, stillness found.
Pines towering, proud and tall,
Guard the silence, embracing all.

Footsteps crunch on the icy floor,
Each step echoes, calling for more.
Nature's blanket, pure and vast,
Holds the warmth of dreams amassed.

Frosted branches arch above,
A symphony of winter's love.
Bright pinpricks against the dark,
Guide lost souls to their spark.

In this realm of shimmering frost,
Those who wander never are lost.
Luminaries in the night sky,
Illuminate paths as stars fly.

The Gaze of Wintry Horizons

Glistening hills stretch far and wide,
Cold winds swirl, on snow they glide.
The horizon's edge, crisp and clear,
Calls the wanderer, drawing near.

Clouds gather, heavy with snow,
Veils of white, a soft, gentle flow.
Beneath the chill, life holds its breath,
In silent wonder, a dance with death.

Sunrise paints the world anew,
Pastel skies with a radiant hue.
Mountains stand with heads held high,
Witnessing time as it passes by.

Birch trees sway in frigid air,
Their branches adorned, a dream laid bare.
Each flake that falls tells a tale,
Of seasons passed and snowy trails.

With every blink, the scene transforms,
Whispers of magic in winter storms.
The gaze of horizons calls to me,
In this stillness, I feel so free.

Frostbitten Whispers of Ancients

Ancient trees hold stories old,
Their bark etched with secrets told.
Frostbitten sighs float through the air,
Echoes of lives that linger there.

Through the mist, shadows appear,
Voices of wisdom, crystal clear.
In the silence, memories hum,
Of distant nights when time was young.

Branches creak, a solemn song,
In the chill of the night, they belong.
Each whispering sound, a timeless trace,
In the heart of winter's embrace.

Beneath the snow, roots intertwine,
Connecting the past, a lifeline divine.
Ancients watch as the cold winds blow,
Guardians of tales buried in snow.

In the frost, a warmth still glows,
In every flake, the ancient prose.
Frostbitten whispers float so high,
Beneath the vast, eternal sky.

Wails of the Blustery Night

The night wails with a howling sound,
Windswept echoes swirl around.
Shadows dance in the moonlit haze,
Immersed in the wild, untamed maze.

Through the trees, a mournful cry,
Stars dim as the clouds sweep by.
Nature's breath, sharp and cold,
Carries stories of the bold.

Forgotten paths in the snow,
Hide where only brave hearts go.
With every gust that chills the bone,
The whispers of the wild are grown.

In the dark, the spirits wander,
Up to the sky, their voices ponder.
Wails of the blustery night, profound,
A symphony of lost, echoing sound.

Yet in this chaos, solace found,
In the rhythm of winter's sound.
Through the tempest, life feels weight,
Wails resonate, a melancholic fate.

Reflections on a Crystal Lake

In the morning light, it gleams,
Mirroring the sky's soft dreams.
Gentle ripples kiss the shore,
Nature whispers, forevermore.

Beneath the surface, secrets hide,
Life dances in its tranquil tide.
A snapshot of the world above,
In silence, finds a hidden love.

Mountains stand in proud array,
Guarding peace at the break of day.
Birds flutter in joyous flight,
Singing tales of the fading night.

Waves embrace the fading glow,
As sun dips low, the waters flow.
A canvas painted by the dawn,
Reflections fade, yet linger on.

The crystal lake, a timeless friend,
Where memories and dreams transcend.
In whispered breeze, life's truths alight,
A haven found in nature's sight.

The Song of the Howling Gale

Through the trees, the wild winds blow,
Singing tales of long ago.
A melody both fierce and free,
The howling gale, a symphony.

It dances wild, it twists and turns,
In its fury, a passion burns.
Echoing through the darkened night,
A voice that roars with deep delight.

Clouds collide as thunder calls,
Nature's music in the squalls.
Each gust, a powerful embrace,
A haunting song that time won't erase.

In shadowed corners, secrets sway,
Guiding dreams that drift away.
The gale's cold breath, both fierce and kind,
A constant force that frees the mind.

As dawn breaks soft on stormy seas,
Calm follows as the spirit frees.
Yet still, the winds will ever wail,
As memories linger in the gale.

Mysteries Woven in Snow

A blanket white upon the ground,
Hushing all, a quiet sound.
In twilight's glow, the world transforms,
As winter's breath, the heart warms.

Footprints tell a tale untold,
Secrets wrapped in silver cold.
Each flake a whisper, soft and bright,
Dancing gently in the light.

Beneath the surface, life does wait,
In icy chamber, unaware of fate.
Nature's lullaby, a deep repose,
Cradled gently in winter's close.

The pines stand tall, their branches bare,
Guarding dreams in frosty air.
Stars peek through, a distant view,
Painting night with colors new.

As dawn awakens, shadows flee,
The mysteries of snow decree.
In every flake, a story flows,
A tapestry of winter's prose.

Echoing Hearts Beneath the Ice

Beneath the surface, hearts entwined,
Whispers carried, love confined.
In frozen depths where dreams reside,
Echoes linger, vast and wide.

Through crystal shards, faint light descends,
Lighting paths where warmth extends.
A pulse beneath, it softly beats,
Resounding through the icy streets.

Silent wishes float like snow,
Promises made beneath the glow.
Each heartbeat is a whispered prayer,
Hoping love will find its air.

The winter's chill cannot erase,
The fire held in love's embrace.
With every thaw, a chance to rise,
To break the silence, touch the skies.

Emerging from the frozen hold,
Hearts are brave, and love is bold.
Echoes fade, yet still they dance,
Beneath the ice, a second chance.

Tales from the Glacial Abyss

In the depths where shadows creep,
Whispers of the cold keep.
A tale of ice, forever bound,
Where ancient secrets, lost, are found.

Silence reigns in frozen halls,
Echoes dance in icy calls.
Mountains guard the silent night,
Stars above, a silver light.

Frosted winds sing lullabies,
Casting dreams beneath the skies.
The abyss holds stories untold,
In glacial tombs, shimmering gold.

From the depths, a ghostly sigh,
Carried on, the spirits fly.
Through the silence, lost we roam,
In this abyss, we find our home.

With each step, the past unfolds,
Tales of bravery, whispers bold.
In the heart of winter's trap,
We find our truth, in silence wrapped.

The Call of the Wild North

Hear the call of the wild north,
Where rugged mountains bring forth.
The howl of wolves fills the air,
A symphony, raw and rare.

Forests whisper in the night,
Under the blanket of moonlight.
Tracks of beasts on the fresh snow,
Tales of journeys, far and slow.

Stars glimmer like ancient gold,
In the darkness, stories unfold.
Nature's heart beats loud and clear,
Echoing what we hold dear.

Rivers run with icy bones,
A melody of nature's tones.
The spirit of the land, alive,
In the wild, we learn to thrive.

In this realm, we roam so free,
Boundless skies and endless sea.
The North calls out, a siren's song,
In this wild, we all belong.

Reflection in a Frozen Lake

Stillness holds the lake in thrall,
Mirrored skies, a perfect call.
Reflections dance with each soft gust,
In the frozen, we place our trust.

Beneath the glass, life's secrets sleep,
In icy depths, memories keep.
Winds weave tales of days gone by,
Whispers caught in the sky.

The sun dips low, a gentle kiss,
Golden rays in the Arctic bliss.
Nature paints with hues so bright,
Capturing the essence of light.

Around the bank, the silence hums,
As nature speaks, the heart succumbs.
In the stillness, peace we find,
A bond so deep, forever entwined.

Frozen whispers, secrets shared,
In the cold, we are laid bare.
The lake reflects both joy and strife,
In its depths, we see our life.

Frostbitten Footprints on Ancient Trails

Footprints lace the frozen earth,
Marking paths of stories worth.
Ancient trails beneath the snow,
Tales of wanderers, long ago.

The frost bites deep, yet we persist,
Every step, a gentle twist.
Echoes of those who walked before,
Guide us to an open door.

Through the woods where shadows play,
We journey forth, come what may.
The spirits linger, wisdom shared,
Along the paths, we are prepared.

Time stands still in winter's grip,
As we navigate this icy trip.
The world in white, a fragile art,
Each footprint tells a beating heart.

Through the cold, our voices sound,
In every flake, laughter is found.
Footprints lead us through the veil,
On ancient trails, we will not fail.

Choreography of the Falling Snow

Delicate flakes spin and sway,
Whirling dancers in the gray.
Softly landing, gentle kiss,
Nature's beauty wrapped in bliss.

Winter's breath upon the trees,
Whispers carried by the breeze.
Each flake tells a silent tale,
Of the world in white, so frail.

In the quiet, peace unfolds,
Frozen wonders, silent molds.
Sparkling dreams in moonlit glow,
Embracing all the falling snow.

Footprints vanish, secrets blend,
Paths of frost that never end.
Every movement, light and free,
In this choreographed decree.

Nature's art, a fleeting grace,
Moments held in winter's embrace.
A soft waltz from earth to sky,
As the snowflakes dance and fly.

The Precipice of Midnight Hues

At the edge where shadows lie,
Midnight whispers, a soft sigh.
Stars are glimmering in the dark,
Painting dreams with every spark.

Silhouettes in twilight's glow,
Colors deep with tales to show.
A canvas vast, a silent tune,
Where the night meets the moon.

Breath of night, a chill embraces,
Echoes haunt these hidden places.
In the silence, hearts unfold,
Secrets spoken, stories told.

The horizon blurs in hues so bright,
Dancing shadows steal the light.
In the depth of night we find,
The beauty forged in the mind.

Standing still at the edge of dreams,
Life is more than what it seems.
In the midnight's gentle grasp,
We hold the beauty, tightly clasp.

Candles of Starlight in the Freeze

Flickering lights in the icy air,
Starlit gems both bright and rare.
Every sparkle tells a wish,
In the night, a sweet, soft bliss.

Frigid breath hangs like a mist,
Hope ignites in every twist.
Candles flicker, shadows play,
Guiding dreams along the way.

In frozen moments, hearts ignite,
Warming footsteps in the night.
Each twinkle, a promise made,
Fading fears that slowly wade.

Gather round the flickered flames,
Whisper softly, share your names.
In this circle, bond and freeze,
Candles of starlight bring us ease.

Both a wonder and a guide,
Glowing softly, side by side.
Starlit candles, in the freeze,
Holding hope in gentle breeze.

A Dance with Frozen Shadows

In the pale light of the dawn,
Frozen shadows stretch and yawn.
Whispers of the night retreat,
As frosty breaths begin to meet.

Every step, a silent glide,
Chasing dreams that roam outside.
The world awakens, still in hush,
Embracing all, no need to rush.

Intricate patterns etched in white,
Dancing softly, hearts take flight.
Weaving stories of the past,
In this moment, hold it fast.

Underneath the frosted trees,
Gentle echoes in the breeze.
Nature's dance, a graceful flow,
A waltz with frozen shadows.

Every twirl, a kiss of cold,
Unwritten tales yet to unfold.
In this fleeting, magic hour,
We find joy in winter's power.

Crystals in the Faded Light

In twilight dreams, the shadows play,
Whispers of night in soft array.
Crystals shimmer, lost in thought,
Echoes of the battles fought.

Glimmers dance on fragile glass,
Moments fleeting, hours pass.
In the silence, stories dwell,
Capturing what words can't tell.

Faded light through branches weaves,
Nature's secret, soft reprieves.
Upon the ground, a fragile trace,
Beauty captured, time's embrace.

Glistening wonders in the gloom,
Silent witnesses in the room.
Every sparkle, every sigh,
Tales of glories, long gone by.

As darkness wraps the world in peace,
Let the haunting whispers cease.
Crystals linger, softly bright,
In the embrace of faded light.

A Frosty Eulogy for the Day

In silence falls the winter's breath,
A shroud of frost, the day meets death.
The sun dips low, a gentle sigh,
As icy whispers bid goodbye.

Barren branches bow in grace,
Crystalline tears upon their face.
The twilight chimes a soft farewell,
In frozen air, a tale to tell.

Snowflakes dance on evening's breath,
A quiet hymn to winter's death.
Each flake a memory, soft and brief,
We mourn the loss, yet find relief.

The horizon glows in pastel shades,
Through frosted fields, the daylight fades.
Each shadow falls, a promise kept,
In this stillness, dreams are swept.

A frost-draped world, serene and deep,
In nature's arms, we find our sleep.
A farewell song upon the night,
A frosty eulogy for the light.

Legends of the Starlit Arctic

Upon the ice, where legends sleep,
The stars above, in silence, weep.
A whispered tale of ages past,
In the Arctic's heart, the die is cast.

Glacial winds hum ancient songs,
Echoing where the spirit belongs.
Beneath the aurora's vibrant veil,
Frosted dreams in winter's trail.

From shadows deep, the wolves will cry,
Guided by the moonlit sky.
Each howl a story, fierce and free,
In harmony with the wild decree.

Crimson skies meet oceans blue,
Where legends wake, as if on cue.
With every twinkle, every sigh,
The Arctic breathes, the stars reply.

In frozen realms, where few have trod,
The spirit dances, an ethereal nod.
Legends forged in icy might,
Live forever in the starlit night.

Soliloquy of the Shivering Trees

In the hush of twilight's grace,
The trees whisper, a solemn place.
With branches bare, they stand and sway,
In memories of warmer days.

Each leaf, a story left behind,
A gentle sigh of the restless mind.
In whispers soft, they seek to share,
The secrets held of earth and air.

They tremble in the evening chill,
A motion sparked by nature's will.
With every crackle, every creak,
The language of the woods they speak.

An old refrain of roots and bark,
In starlit nights or when it's dark.
A chorus sung in haunting tones,
The trees remember all alone.

In every sway, a tale unfolds,
Of whispered dreams and ancient old.
The soliloquy of shivering trees,
A testament to life's decrees.

A Lament for the Frozen Shore

Upon the ice, the silence reigns,
Whispers of dreams lost to the chains.
Waves that once sang a joy-laden tune,
Now merely echo beneath the cold moon.

Footprints of past in crystals now tread,
Memories linger where warmth has fled.
The sea, a mirror for the heart's despair,
Reflects the hopes that floated in air.

Beneath the frost, a world sleeps in pain,
Cracked shells of sunlight, all but a stain.
Shores that once danced with life's sweet embrace,
Now hold a stillness, a vacant space.

Grit of the sand, frozen in time,
Melting to echoes that fade into rhyme.
Each gust of wind bears a sorrowful tune,
A lament for the lost, beneath the pale moon.

Murmurs from the Northern Skies

Stars twinkle softly like secrets in flight,
Caressed by the shadows of the deep night.
Whispers of ancients drift low like a sigh,
Calling the hearts that once dared to fly.

Northern lights shimmer, a dance so divine,
Painting the heavens with colors that shine.
Each flicker of brilliance tells tales from afar,
Woven in dreams, like the path of a star.

Through the cold winds, a melody flows,
Serenading silence where the midnight rose.
Voices of ages, through the frost they speak,
Carrying wisdom for the willing and weak.

In the quiet of night, let your spirit unfold,
Embrace the whispers that the heavens hold.
For in the stillness, connections are made,
Murmurs from the skies, where the heart won't fade.

Glimmers of Distant Stars

In the vast expanse, where dreams take flight,
Glimmers of stars shyly pierce the night.
Each shining beacon tells tales of the past,
Of wanderers lost and the shadows they've cast.

Light-years away, but their glow still aligns,
Guiding the hearts where the mystery shines.
Constellations whisper in a language so true,
Mapping the journeys that once they knew.

Caught in the web of the celestial sphere,
Echoes of laughter rise up like a tear.
Moments of joy, in the starlight they dwell,
Glimmers of hope in a universe swell.

Hold fast to the light of these distant dreams,
Life flows in currents, like beautiful streams.
For even in darkness, when shadows arise,
Glimmers remain in our hearts like the skies.

Songs of the Shimmering Frost

The frost paints the world in a delicate hue,
Lending its brilliance to moments anew.
Each flake that descends holds a song in its grace,
Whispering secrets of time's gentle face.

In the early dawn, when the silence takes hold,
A symphony stirs, in the air it unfolds.
With laughter of snowflakes, the branches are kissed,
Nature's soft chorus, too pure to be missed.

Songs echo softly in the crisp winter air,
Resonating warmth in the chill's gentle stare.
Every note dances in crystalline light,
The shimmering frost sings of day after night.

So let us rejoice in the magic we find,
In songs that surround us, like threads intertwined.
For life is a melody, both fleeting and fast,
A tapestry woven, in the present and past.

Footprints in the Silent Snow

In the hush of winter's grace,
Footprints trace a distant place.
Whispers softly through the air,
Nature's secrets hidden there.

Blankets white on earth's embrace,
Each step tells a timeless tale.
Silent echoes, soft and sweet,
History beneath our feet.

Glistening stars in the night sky,
Look above, let your heart fly.
Every shadow speaks of dreams,
In moonlight, all is as it seems.

Winds of winter carry cheer,
With each footfall, cast off fear.
Silent paths lead me away,
Into night, into the day.

Snowflakes dance on winds so clear,
Footprints vanish year by year.
Yet the heart holds on so tight,
To those paths of purest light.

Lanterns of the Arctic Night

In the vast and icy deep,
Lanterns flicker, secrets keep.
Illuminating frozen dreams,
Glowing softly, shadowed beams.

Stars like jewels in the sky,
Winking down as time slips by.
Whispers of the morning light,
Dance with shadows of the night.

Icebergs shine, a crystal glow,
Nature's art, a stunning show.
Echoes of the past still roam,
In the night, they find a home.

Hushed are all the fleeting sounds,
In the darkness, magic bounds.
Lanterns guide, a gentle flame,
In the cold, we share the same.

With each breath, the world awakes,
As the morning softly breaks.
Lanterns dim, yet hearts stay bright,
Chasing dreams in Arctic night.

Drifting Dreams on the Winter Breeze

Whispers carried on the air,
Drifting dreams without a care.
Snowflakes twirl, a soft ballet,
Guiding thoughts to light the way.

In the quiet, still and deep,
Nature sings us all to sleep.
Crystals spark as shadows fall,
Winter's echo, a gentle call.

Frozen branches, lace of white,
Decorate the starry night.
Beneath the moon, we softly tread,
Following the dreams we've said.

Through the chill, our spirits soar,
Seeking warmth forevermore.
Every sigh, a breath of peace,
In this moment, all release.

Softly now, the night grows old,
Stories whispered, tales retold.
Drifting dreams on winter's breeze,
In this magic, find your ease.

The Call of the Wild North

Echoes through the towering pines,
The wild north, where nature shines.
Mountains rise with majesty,
Calling hearts to roam so free.

Rivers rush with icy flow,
Underneath the moon's soft glow.
Whispers of the earth's heartbeat,
Guide us on with every beat.

In the twilight, shadows creep,
As the world begins to sleep.
Stars awaken, bright and bold,
Telling stories long since told.

Fires crackle, warmth unfolds,
The north's embrace, a tale of gold.
Winds that whisper through the night,
Carry dreams beyond our sight.

The call of wild, fierce and true,
In this land, we start anew.
Every path, a tale to find,
In the north, we leave behind.

Ink on a Frozen Canvas

Ink drips from the quill,
Spreading dreams so grand,
Lines carve through the frost,
On this silent land.

Whispers of the night,
Dance upon the air,
Each word a snowflake,
Gentle and rare.

Stars glitter above,
A cosmic embrace,
Sketching tales of old,
In this boundless space.

Thoughts swirl like the snow,
Softly they arrive,
Painting life anew,
While the world's alive.

This canvas holds more,
Than what eyes can see,
Frozen ink and hope,
Set the spirit free.

Songs Carried by the Winter Wind

The wind carries songs,
Through the barren trees,
Echoes of lost hopes,
Floating with the breeze.

Chill bites at the skin,
Yet warmth lies within,
Notes blend with the night,
As new tales begin.

Harmonies of past,
Whisper through the dark,
Each note like a star,
Longing for a spark.

As frosty breath swirls,
In this quiet space,
Dreams dance on the wind,
Wearing winter's grace.

In the hearts of all,
These melodies breathe,
Songs of winter's truth,
In the cold we cleave.

Reverie of the Endless Night

Night falls like a cloak,
Softly it enfolds,
Whispers in the dark,
Secrets to be told.

Stars blink like lanterns,
Guiding lost souls' flight,
In this endless realm,
Of shadow and light.

Moonlight bathes the earth,
Casting silvery beams,
Carving paths of dreams,
In our midnight schemes.

Silence holds a song,
Sung by hidden things,
Echoes of the heart,
Where the nightbird sings.

In reverie we drift,
On horizons wide,
Wrapped in starlit hope,
With the moon as guide.

Lullabies of the Snowy Plains

Across the snowy plains,
Lullabies gently sigh,
Wrapped in winter's arms,
Where all dreams can lie.

Soft flakes kiss the earth,
Cradling weary hearts,
Singing through the night,
As the stillness starts.

A hush blankets all,
In this tranquil space,
Each whisper of snow,
A warm, sweet embrace.

Underneath the stars,
The world slows its pace,
With lullabies sung,
In a soft, white lace.

Rest now, weary souls,
In the frost you'll find,
A lullaby's gift,
Gentle and kind.

Haiku of the Icy Streams

Whispers of the frost,
Beneath the crystal veil,
Streams weave through the pines,
Nature's frozen breath.

Sunlight breaks the chill,
Dancing on the surface,
Life stirs in slow wake,
A timid rebirth.

Soundless, pure and bright,
Life held in glacial pause,
Time flows like the ice,
Eternity's touch.

Echoes of the past,
Footprints on the white shore,
Fleeting as the melt,
Whispers fade away.

Solstice Shadows Over Silent Valleys

Golden light descends,
Shadows stretch and linger,
Valleys breathe in peace,
Time graced by stillness.

Breezes softly hum,
Carrying secrets old,
Over hills they glide,
Embracing the dusk.

In the fading glow,
Nature holds its breath tight,
Crickets serenade,
Night's gentle embrace.

Stars begin to wake,
Painting dreams in the dark,
Hope flickers like flames,
Guiding wandering hearts.

Silent breath of night,
Whispers of the cosmos,
Cradled in the dark,
Awaiting the dawn.

The Muse of Northern Horizons

A canvas of dreams,
Painted in twilight hues,
Northern lights ignite,
Imagination's spark.

Whispers in the winds,
Calling forth the unseen,
Guiding starry souls,
To lands yet unknown.

Mountains loom so tall,
Crowned in glistening white,
Echoes of the muse,
Dance upon the peaks.

Hearts beat in rhythm,
With the pulse of the earth,
Awakening dreams,
In the still of night.

Infinite expanse,
Wrapped in mystery's cloak,
Horizons unfold,
In endless embrace.

Lullaby of the Falling Snow

Gentle flakes descend,
Whispers of winter's hush,
Cradled on the wind,
Softly falling dreams.

Nature sighs in peace,
Blanketing the cold earth,
Silent symphony,
As time drifts away.

Children's laughter rings,
Chasing snowflakes around,
Joy wrapped in white dust,
Hearts warmed by the light.

Stars twinkle above,
Guiding the slumbering night,
With dreams intertwined,
In the cradle of snow.

Morning breaks the spell,
Sunlight kisses the frost,
In this quiet dawn,
The world breathes anew.

Stories Carved in Glacial Stone

Silent heights that touch the skies,
Beneath the frost, a tale lies.
Each crevice holds a whispered story,
Chiseled deep in icy glory.

Time stands still where shadows creep,
In glacial hearts, the secrets keep.
The world will fade, but stones remain,
Guardians of the frozen pain.

Waves of ice and crystal clear,
Echoes of the past draw near.
With every thaw, a voice revealed,
History's grip forever sealed.

Nature's art in muted hues,
Ancient myths in silver blues.
In every flake, a story glows,
Woven tight in winter's throes.

As glaciers shift, new tales arise,
In sacred silence, wisdom lies.
Bound by time, but ever free,
Legends carved, for all to see.

Chasing the Frigid Dream

In the twilight's soft embrace,
Chasing dreams through winter's grace.
Footsteps crunch on powdered snow,
Where only whispers dare to go.

Stars above in frozen dance,
In their light, we dare to prance.
The night holds secrets, vast and wide,
In frosted breath, we dream and ride.

Moonlit paths that lead us on,
In the stillness, fears are gone.
With every chill, our spirits rise,
Chasing warmth beneath the skies.

The frigid air, a gentle kiss,
In each moment, find your bliss.
Winds of winter sing a tune,
Beneath the watchful, silver moon.

Awakened hearts in icy fields,
To the chill, our passion yields.
In the cold, we find our flame,
Chasing dreams, we know no shame.

Whispers of the Boreal Forest

In the glade where shadows dwell,
Boreal sighs weave magic's spell.
Tall pines stand with stories old,
Whispers dance in winds so bold.

Mossy carpets guard the ground,
In hush of night, secrets found.
Creatures scurry, hearts attune,
To the pulse beneath the moon.

Snowflakes lace the quiet air,
Each a wish, floating without care.
In nature's vault, time's a friend,
In its embrace, all sorrows mend.

Branches drape with icy threads,
Covering all in silver spreads.
Listen close, the forest sighs,
In its breath, the past still flies.

Echoes cradle every sound,
In this sanctuary found.
Let the whispers guide your way,
Through the night, into the day.

Harmony of the Frozen Silence

In the land where ice confides,
Harmony in stillness bides.
Each flake falls like a gentle note,
In a symphony, the cold devotes.

Frosted glass on branches cling,
Nature's breath begins to sing.
Silent chords in moonlit night,
Wrap us in their soft delight.

The world slows down, a breath held tight,
In frozen air, all feels right.
Moments linger, unhurried pace,
In the silence, find your space.

Echoes paste of times long gone,
Yet in this song, we carry on.
With each stillness, peace is found,
In the quiet, hearts abound.

Harmony sings through every flake,
In the stillness, our hearts awake.
Together woven, night and day,
In frozen silence, we shall stay.

Lament of the Flickering Flame

In the darkness, shadows dance,
A flickering flame, a fleeting chance.
Whispers echo, tales of old,
Of warmth forgotten, stories cold.

Once a beacon, now subdued,
In the silence, solitude brewed.
Fragile embers, hopes ignite,
Yet darkness looms, consuming light.

Memories haunt, they rise and fall,
The crackling voice, a ghostly call.
Each flicker tells of time gone by,
As shadows stretch, like a sigh.

Yearning for the glow to stay,
The warmth that fades, just slips away.
In fragile hands, the fire's breath,
A dance with life, a waltz with death.

So I mourn this dwindling spark,
A flickering flame in the dark.
Hold it close, lest it flee,
A lament for what used to be.

Messages Carried on Glacial Breezes

Whispers float on icy air,
Carried soft, like a lover's dare.
Secrets drift, a gentle sigh,
Beneath the vast, unyielding sky.

Untouched lands, a frozen maze,
Nature's breath in silent praise.
Echoes linger, tales unfold,
In crystal shards, their whispers told.

Shimmering flakes that gleam at night,
Dancing softly in silver light.
They hold the dreams of distant lands,
Glistening hopes in frozen strands.

A heart attuned to nature's song,
Feels the pull of a world so long.
Each chill breeze, a haunting tale,
Of love and loss on winter's trail.

Through glacial whispers, spirits roam,
In every flake, a hint of home.
Messages carried, soft yet clear,
Reaching hearts both far and near.

The Poetry of Ice and Snow

A tapestry of white and blue,
Nature's canvas, a vibrant hue.
Each flake unique, a work of art,
Crafted softly, a silent start.

Silent moments, frozen dreams,
Reflecting light in gentle beams.
Whispers echo through the pines,
In the hush, a world that shines.

Snowflakes dance on winter's breath,
A fleeting touch, a hint of death.
Yet in their fall, life's joy remains,
As nature weeps, yet blooms again.

Icicles hanging, sharp and bright,
Catch the sun in fleeting light.
Nature's breath, a fragile state,
In the poetry, we contemplate.

Beneath the snow, life stirs below,
A promise kept beneath the glow.
In every drift, a tale is spun,
Of ice and snow, where all begun.

Beneath the Gaze of Winter's Moon

Under the moon's cold, silver gaze,
   Winter stretches in quiet ways.
Stars twinkle like diamonds rare,
   In the stillness, hearts lay bare.

The world sleeps deep in snowy shrouds,
   Wrapped in blankets, silent clouds.
Dreams take flight in the frosty air,
   While shadows whisper, unaware.

Footsteps crunch on the frozen ground,
   In the silence, a yearning sound.
Nature holds its breath in awe,
   A sacred moment, a peaceful draw.

Branches glisten with icy lace,
   Under the moon's enchanted grace.
Each night unfolds a new tale spun,
   As winter dances with the sun.

Here beneath the winter's eye,
   Life pauses, a tranquil sigh.
In stillness, beauty finds its tune,
   Beneath the gaze of winter's moon.

Beneath the Boughs of Ancient Fir Trees

Shadows dance in filtered light,
Wisps of green, a tranquil sight.
Roots entwined, a whispered tale,
In nature's heart, the wild prevails.

Gentle breezes weave their song,
In this place where we belong.
Mossy carpets, whispers clear,
The ancient firs hold all we fear.

Time is still, the world abates,
In boughs where silence percolates.
Healing thoughts like branches rise,
Underneath the stretching skies.

Beams of sun and shadows play,
A fragrant hearth where spirits sway.
Each moment savored, deeply found,
A sanctuary in the ground.

Beneath the boughs where life begins,
And dances softly in the winds.
A refuge carved from earth and tree,
In harmony, we are set free.

Tides of Whispering Winds

Winds caress the rolling hills,
Brushing through with gentle thrills.
Whispers weave through branches high,
Singing secrets from the sky.

Tides of air, they ebb and flow,
Carrying dreams, both fast and slow.
Notes of nature, pure and bright,
Dancing in the pale moonlight.

Echoes linger where they roam,
Every gust feels like a home.
They cradle soft the weary heart,
A melody, a brand new start.

Through valleys deep and mountains wide,
The winds, they whisper, never hide.
In the stillness, tales unwind,
A journey shared, a bond that binds.

So let us listen with intent,
To the voices that the breezes sent.
In every sigh and every breath,
We find the strength to dance with death.

Chasing Echoes Across Frozen Fens

Crystals glint upon the frost,
Silent whispers of the lost.
Footsteps crunch on icy grounds,
Mysteries in silence found.

Beneath the moon's pale, silver glow,
Shadows dance, with secrets in tow.
Echoes calling through the night,
Chasing dreams in frozen flight.

Rippling waters, now asleep,
Guarding stories we cannot keep.
In the stillness, echoes rise,
Reflections drawn from deep blue skies.

Windows to a frozen past,
Moments linger, shadows cast.
Voices flutter like a sigh,
Chasing echoes, we ask why.

Across the fens, the cold winds sweep,
Inviting thoughts that cut so deep.
Amidst the chill, we're not alone,
In nature's court, we find our own.

Soliloquy of Polar Silence

In the heart of ice, a calm prevails,
Frozen whispers weave their tales.
The world outside a distant hum,
In solitude, our thoughts succumb.

Silent crystals catch the light,
Creating prisms, a haunting sight.
Each moment stretches, vast and wide,
A canvas pure with nothing to hide.

Beneath the stars, the silence sings,
As frostbite kisses earthy rings.
In solitude, we find our peace,
In frozen realms, all worries cease.

The weight of winter, calm yet bold,
Stories whisper, secrets told.
Reflections dance on quiet snows,
In this stillness, beauty grows.

In polar silence, thoughts take flight,
Reaching deep into the night.
Where echoes linger, and hearts remain,
In solitude, we find our gain.

Echoes from the Icebound Lakes

Beneath the frost, the water sleeps,
Whispers linger, secrets deep.
Shrouded in crystals, time stands still,
Nature's heart beats with icy thrill.

Mountains mirror the frozen glow,
Silent witnesses to tales of snow.
Echoes call from shores once bare,
In winter's grasp, we find our prayer.

Wisps of mist dance on the edge,
As shadows dip and softly pledge.
The stars reflect in liquid glass,
Each ripple holds the moments past.

Cold winds weave their haunting thread,
Through icy realms where fears have bled.
Yet warmth resides within the soul,
As stories weave to make us whole.

Embrace the quiet, heed the call,
In icebound lakes, we find our all.
Through frozen dreams, we journey far,
Guided by the northern star.

Legends of the Wind-Scarred Peaks

High above the valleys wide,
Where eagles soar and dreams reside.
The whispering winds tell tales of old,
Of brave hearts and treasures untold.

Rugged cliffs, they tower high,
Kissing clouds that drift on by.
Each stone holds a story rare,
Of ancients who once lingered there.

Through tempest storms and lightning's flash,
The peaks stand firm, a steadfast clash.
Legends born from trials faced,
In nature's arms, the future traced.

From valleys low to summits grand,
Every footstep, a tale so planned.
The wind, it sings through every crack,
A timeless echo we can't turn back.

In shadows cast, the moments freeze,
Bolts of courage riding the breeze.
In the heights where spirits sing,
The heart of adventure takes to wing.

Secrets in the Northern Nightingale's Song

In the hush of twilight's sigh,
Nightingales weave a lullaby.
Softly hidden in twilight's cloak,
Their melodies gently evoke.

Amidst the pines, the secrets dwell,
In every note, a timeless spell.
Whispers carried on the breeze,
Caught in the rustle of the leaves.

Their songs, a map of realms obscure,
Where dreams and hopes align for sure.
A tapestry of starlit skies,
As night unveils its mystic ties.

Listen close to the tales they spin,
Of love and loss, where hearts begin.
In the shadows, stories intertwine,
Through every note, the stars align.

The northern winds embrace the night,
Guiding lost souls toward the light.
In the beauty of their song, we find,
A reflection of the heart and mind.

Twilight's Embrace in Whispering Woods

As daylight fades, the woods awake,
In twilight's glow, new pathways take.
Whispers dance through branches bare,
Secrets shared with the cool night air.

A gentle breeze, a soft caress,
Each rustle holds a sweet abyss.
In shadows deep, the magic weaves,
Where dreams take flight and hope believes.

With every step, the echoes call,
The heart of nature welcomes all.
Moonlight paints a silver trace,
In the woods, we find our place.

Each twilight hour holds stories bright,
Of creatures that roam in the night.
The owls watch with knowing eyes,
As starlit paths lead to the skies.

Embraced by peace, beneath the trees,
We find our solace, pray with ease.
In whispering woods, we drift along,
In twilight's arms, we find our song.

Echoes Beneath the Frozen Canopy

Beneath the frost, whispers roam,
Through silent woods, they find their home.
Frozen branches softly sway,
In the hush of winter's play.

Footprints trace a path unknown,
A dance of shadows, softly grown.
In the stillness, echoes call,
Nature's secrets, one and all.

Moonlight casts a pale, bright glow,
Illuminating all below.
Each breath a cloud, cold and white,
As stars emerge to greet the night.

The nightingale sings her tune,
To the rhythm of the moon.
Echoes linger in the air,
A melody beyond compare.

In this realm of dreams and sighs,
Magic lingers, never dies.
Underneath the frozen trees,
Whispers dance upon the breeze.

Shadows of the Old Cedar

In the forest, tall and grand,
Cedar whispers, soft and bland.
Roots that grasp the earth with grace,
Shadows deepen, time can't erase.

With each season, stories weave,
In the bark, the tales believe.
Ravens caw, echoing lore,
Of ancient days that came before.

The wind carries secrets near,
In every rustle, tales appear.
Life abounds amidst the still,
Nature's pulse, a silent thrill.

Branches stretch to touch the sky,
Underneath, the moments fly.
In the shade, lost thoughts abide,
In the peace, the heart can hide.

Roots entwined beneath the ground,
In quiet solitude, we're found.
Cedar stands through time and strife,
A witness to the dance of life.

Echoing Silence in Winter's Grasp

Winter's chill holds lands in thrall,
Echoing silence, nature's call.
Softly, softly, the snowflakes fall,
A tranquil blanket, life at stall.

Footsteps crunch on paths of white,
Underneath the pale moonlight.
In the stillness, dreams take flight,
Wrapped in the cloak of endless night.

Branches bend with frosty weight,
Time slows down, a measured fate.
In the hush, secrets unfold,
Stories of the brave and bold.

Amidst the cold, a fire glows,
In warming hearts, the spirit flows.
Embers dance, casting light,
Against the shadows of the night.

In echoing silence, peace resounds,
In winter's grasp, true beauty found.
Nature cradles life anew,
In every breath, the world feels true.

Starry Veil of the Northern Night

Underneath the starry dome,
Northern lights begin to roam.
Colors dance in radiant arcs,
Painting skies, igniting sparks.

Whispers of the cosmic show,
Breeze that sings of worlds below.
Time stands still as dreams ignite,
In the magic of the night.

Mountains rise against the glow,
In the silence, secrets flow.
Each twinkle holds a story near,
Waiting for the heart to hear.

Frozen lakes reflect the sky,
Mirroring the stars up high.
Nature's quilt, a wondrous sight,
Bathed in beams of silver light.

As dawn creeps with soft caress,
Night retreats, a wakefulness.
Yet in dreams, the stars remain,
A memory that will sustain.

Echos of Solitude in the Chilling Night

Whispers linger in the air,
Lost voices fill the gloom.
Stars above, a distant flare,
Silence holds the moon's loom.

Footsteps soft on ancient ground,
Night wraps all in its embrace.
Each heartbeat is a ghostly sound,
Time dances without a trace.

Shadows weave through twisted trees,
Darkness swallows all that's bright.
A chill wraps like a gentle breeze,
In solitude's quiet night.

Thoughts drift like autumn leaves,
Falling softly, ever near.
In the stillness, heart believes,
Hope survives through silent fear.

Yet in this vast and empty space,
A flicker warms the heart's plea.
Echos linger, find their place,
In the calm, we feel so free.

Frosty Gaze of the Distant Peaks

Mountains stand so pure and grand,
Tops adorned with sparkling snow.
Whispers carried by the wind,
Stories of the ages flow.

Every peak a silent guard,
Watching over time's embrace.
Nature's bounty, steadily hard,
Holding secrets in their grace.

Underneath the crystal sky,
Frosty breath on bundled skin.
Paths ahead, like dreams, they fly,
Where adventures can begin.

A gaze that pierces through the cold,
Inviting hearts to roam and seek.
Echoes of the brave and bold,
Underneath the world's mystique.

In the dawn, the light breaks through,
Painting peaks with blush of fire.
A frosty gaze, so pure and true,
Filling souls with wild desire.

Fireside Songs of the North's Heart

Crackling flames dance in the night,
Stories spun within the glow.
Voices rise with pure delight,
Fireside warmth in winter's flow.

Each tale a thread, woven tight,
Binding hearts in laughter's thrall.
Memories share their vibrant light,
Flickering shadows on the wall.

A harmony of old and new,
With every song, spirits soar.
In the North where dreams come true,
The fires speak forevermore.

The chill outside fades to mere breath,
As we gather, close and dear.
In this moment, life defies death,
Held by warmth, love conquers fear.

With every note, the night ignites,
Echoes cruel winds far away.
Fireside songs, a beacon bright,
Guide us through the night and day.

Murmuring Rivers and Wandering Winds

Rivers weave through valleys deep,
Carving tales where time stands still.
Murmurs soft that never sleep,
Whispers of a world to fill.

Wandering winds, they laugh and play,
Caressing leaves with gentle grace.
Their lullabies drift far away,
A timeless song that time won't chase.

Each twist and turn, a secret shared,
Flowing freely, wild and true.
Nature's breath, a bond declared,
Where dreams are born and skies are blue.

Underneath the swaying trees,
Harmony of earth and air.
Dancing lightly on the breeze,
Life unfolds beyond compare.

Golden sun and silver moon,
Reflections dance on water's face.
Murmuring rivers, winds that croon,
Together weave a sweet embrace.

Dances of the Northern Lights

In shimmering green and vibrant blue,
The heavens sway in a cosmic hue.
They twirl and twist in icy air,
Whispers of magic, everywhere.

Stars come alive, a flickering dance,
A celestial waltz, a dreamlike trance.
Under the gaze of the moonlit sky,
Nature's ballet, enchanting the eye.

Beneath the auroras, the night ignites,
Fires of wonder, sparkling lights.
They guide the lost, they dazzle the bold,
Stories of beauty, in silence told.

With each flutter, the darkness retreats,
Revealing a world where magic meets.
The dance goes on in silence profound,
In the embrace of the ethereal sound.

So let us marvel, let us behold,
The dances of light, a sight to unfold.
In the northern skies, we find our way,
Amidst the splendor, we long to stay.

Shadows on an Endless Tundra

Whispers of wind on a frozen plain,
Footsteps echo, a soft refrain.
Shadows stretch where the daylight fades,
An endless canvas, of twilight shades.

Lonely hills beneath the starry veil,
Stories linger in the icy trail.
A silence deep as the midnight sea,
As nature holds her breath, so free.

The tundra breathes with a tranquil might,
As shadows play in the fading light.
Under the blanket of endless snow,
The heart beats softly, a gentle flow.

Each star above, a watchful eye,
Gazing down where the spirits lie.
They dance with shadows, both dark and bright,
In the hushed whispers of the endless night.

So roam the tundra, where silence sings,
In the twilight's grip, the world takes wings.
Embrace the shadows that gently roam,
For in their depth, you may find home.

Voices in the Cold Twilight

In the hush of dusk, where whispers blend,
Voices emerge, like dear old friends.
They weave through the snow, a gentle call,
Echoes of winter, embracing all.

They speak of journeys on frozen trails,
Of ancient tales where the heart prevails.
Stories of snowflakes and silent nights,
Of distant stars and glowing lights.

In cold twilight, the air is clear,
Each voice a melody that we hold dear.
The frost-kissed ground beneath our feet,
Hums to the rhythm of nature's beat.

Listen closely, you might just find,
A secret language that's intertwined.
Whispers of earth, sky, and sea,
In the cold twilight, we are set free.

So gather the voices that boldly sing,
In the twilight's arms, let your heart take wing.
In echoes of winter, we embrace the night,
Where every shadow becomes a light.

Tales from the Luminous North

In the luminous glow of the polar night,
Tales unfurl in the silver light.
Stories of frost and the howling wind,
Of ancient spirits that still transcend.

The northern lights weave a cloak so bright,
Each tale a shadow, a flicker of light.
They speak of dreams, both bold and fair,
Carried by winds that whisper their prayer.

From mountain peaks to valleys deep,
In every silence, the secrets keep.
A tapestry of history brightly spun,
Of love, of loss, and battles won.

Gather the stories as they unfold,
In the shimmering night, warm and cold.
Each heartbeat echoes through time and space,
In the luminous north, we find our place.

So let the tales from the north ignite,
The spirit within on this starry night.
For in every story, a part of us glows,
In the luminous north, where wonder flows.

Harmony of the Icy Whirlpools

In the depths, the currents play,
Whispers of the water sway,
Frosty tendrils intertwine,
Nature's pulse, a soft design.

Broken ice like diamonds shine,
Glimmers dance on frozen lines,
Each turn a symphony calls,
Echoes in the silence fall.

Whirlpools twist with graceful ease,
Flowing through the sturdy trees,
Cold embrace of winter's art,
A tranquil balm to every heart.

Underneath the silver sky,
Where time pauses, and dreams lie,
Harmony of peace prevails,
In the icy, swirling trails.

Crystals float on air so light,
Painting scenes of pure delight,
Nature's brush, a wondrous sight,
In the whirlpools, day and night.

Reflections of a Frosted Heart

Within the frost, a shadow glows,
Silent whispers, soft and slow,
Glasslike echoes on the ground,
In stillness, all is profound.

Every flake, a story told,
In icy words, the past unfolds,
Twinkling lights reflect the face,
Of a heart in quiet grace.

Gentle currents sweep the soul,
Winter's hand makes broken whole,
In the depths, a warmth ignites,
Frosted dreams, like stars, take flight.

Mirrored in the calm of night,
Shadows dance in silver light,
Every heartbeat whispers low,
Reflections of the falling snow.

A frosted heart finds its way,
Through the chill of winter's sway,
In every breath, a song begins,
The cycle of life, it spins.

Silence of the Winter's Breath

A hush envelops earth and sky,
As winter whispers softly by,
Blankets of white cloak the trees,
In the stillness, hearts find peace.

Snowflakes drift like whispered prayers,
Falling gently, light as air,
In the quiet, time slows down,
Nature wears her frosted crown.

Echoes lost in frozen air,
Each moment, heavy with care,
The world breathes in soft refrain,
A symphony of cold and rain.

Silence speaks in shades of gray,
While shadows softly sway,
Winter's breath, a soothing balm,
Embracing all with gentle calm.

In the dark, a flicker glows,
Underneath the soft white snows,
Silence of the winter's breath,
A dance of life beyond the death.

Whispers of the Frigid Winds

Through the trees, the cold winds sigh,
Tales of winter passing by,
Each gust a feathered caress,
In the chill, the heart can rest.

Whispers weave through icy boughs,
Nature bows and softly vows,
Telling secrets to the night,
In the dark, the stars ignite.

Frigid touch on cheeks so warm,
Taking form as winter's charm,
Every note a gentle tease,
In the air, a symphony frees.

Winds of change, they come and go,
Marking seasons in their flow,
Chilling laughter on the breeze,
Life awakes with frosty ease.

Every breath a frozen dream,
In the night, where shadows gleam,
Whispers of the frigid winds,
Where every tale of winter begins.

Hushed Stories Beneath the Stars

In the stillness of night, whispers gleam,
Tales of the cosmos, soft as a dream.
Echoes of laughter, floating in air,
Holding the secrets that night stars share.

Crickets are singing, a rhythmic grace,
Moonlight illuminating each hidden space.
Constellations twinkle, guiding with pride,
Light-years apart, yet never divide.

The world pauses soft, in the starry glow,
Each flicker of light, a story to show.
Voices long gone, yet the night does recall,
Binding the past with the present for all.

Glimmers of hope in the darkest skies,
Every star shines bright, despite the goodbyes.
Hearts intertwined, beneath the vast sea,
Embracing the stillness where we long to be.

A canvas of dreams, painted with grace,
As time melts away, in this tranquil space.
Forever we'll treasure, these stories untold,
Hushed under stars, our hearts they behold.

Remnants of an Icy Past

Beneath the blanket of winter's chill,
Memories linger, strong and still.
Frozen whispers, time's gentle brush,
Echoes of moments in the quiet hush.

Rivers once flowed, now encased in white,
Sketches of warmth in the pale moonlight.
With each day's dawn, the frost starts to flee,
Revealing the tales of what used to be.

Icicles dangling, sharp as a knife,
Carving the remnants of seasons of life.
The silent forests, a nostalgic sigh,
Where shadows of laughter seem to pass by.

Buried in snow, stories await,
Held by the frost, sealed fate after fate.
Yet spring will cradle what winter has claimed,
And warmth will return, though nothing's the same.

Echoing memories, through frost they are cast,
Remnants of beauty, a glimpse of the past.
Nature's own canvas, an artful display,
Whispers of winter, fading away.

Frosted Petals on a Silent Breeze

Delicate petals kissed by the cold,
Whispers of beauty, timeless and bold.
Frost as a veil, softening each hue,
Nature's soft palette in glistening dew.

As silence prevails, all seems so still,
The breath of the earth, a gentle thrill.
Under the moonlight, each flower glows,
Treasures of winter, in graceful repose.

Wind carries secrets through branches bare,
A dance of frost, so light and rare.
The hush of the night, a delicate art,
Frosted dreams weave through the heart.

Crystals that shimmer like stars on the ground,
Softly they whisper, a tranquil sound.
Capturing moments in fragile dreams,
Frosted petals whisper of timeless themes.

With dawn on the horizon, warmth will return,
But in this stillness, our spirits will yearn.
For beauty like this, oh how it can please,
Frosted petals drifting on a silent breeze.

Echoing Cries of the Arctic Fox

In the moonlit night, a shadow takes flight,
The softly padded paws, a glimmer of white.
Echoes surround, as the silence breaks,
The haunting calls of the fox, it wakes.

Through the frozen tundra, it gracefully roams,
An artist of stealth, making icy homes.
Every call a story, every trail a thread,
Woven through winter, where secrets are bred.

Stars blanket the sky, flickering keen,
Guiding the fox through this silent scene.
Its breath, a soft mist in the crisp, cold air,
A spirit of wilderness, noble and rare.

The echoing cries, they ripple through night,
Resonating deep, in the stillness of flight.
With each distant howl, the wild comes alive,
In the heart of the frost, where echoes survive.

As dawn's first light breaks the shadowy gloom,
The echoes will fade, but their essence will bloom.
An arctic tale, whispered wide and far,
The echoing cries of each heartbound star.

Frost-Kissed Memories of Yore

In the hush of morning's glow,
Footprints in the fading snow,
Whispers of a time gone by,
Beneath the pale and silent sky.

Echoes of laughter drift so clear,
Framed by the chill, they disappear,
Wrapped in warmth of tales retold,
Frost-kissed dreams, a sight to behold.

Branches heavy, burdened with ice,
Nature's jewels, oh, so precise,
Memories cling like winter's breath,
Silent songs of life and death.

As shadows dance in twilight's shade,
Remnants of youth in the cold cascade,
Each flake a story lost in time,
Fleeting moments, so sublime.

Through blizzards fierce and skies so gray,
We find our light in the darkest day,
With every breath, a prayer we send,
In frost-kissed memories, we transcend.

A Prayer to the Northern Skies

Beneath the vast and starry dome,
We lift our hearts, far from home,
In silence, we whisper our dreams,
Under the glow of silver beams.

O northern lights, dance so bright,
Guide our souls through the endless night,
With every flicker, every hue,
A prayer flows to the heavens blue.

Snowflakes fall like silent sighs,
Each one a wish that gently flies,
Carried on the crisp, cold air,
To find the hope resting somewhere.

Embers glowing in the dark,
Spark a warmth, a hidden spark,
Let every heart reach for the skies,
Where dreams take root and never die.

So here we stand, in the frozen light,
With hopes that shimmer, burning bright,
A prayer enfolded in winter's lore,
To the northern skies, forevermore.

Dreams in Icy Reflections

Upon the lake, a mirror bright,
Reflecting dreams in the pale moonlight,
Icy whispers of what could be,
In the stillness, I long to be free.

Each crystal shard tells a tale,
Of winter's breath and winds that wail,
Caught in time, like echoes in glass,
Dreams woven softly, moments amassed.

The frozen world, a quiet friend,
Whispers softly, will you transcend?
In every shimmer, a truth unfolds,
As life unwinds, the future holds.

Footsteps tread on the icy shore,
Awakening dreams, forevermore,
With every glance at the frigid lake,
A chance to mend, a path to make.

So hold these dreams, let them unfurl,
In icy reflections, a hidden pearl,
For in the stillness of the night,
We find our way, toward the light.

The Silence of Winter's Breath

In the stillness, a quiet call,
Winter's breath envelops all,
Softly falling, the snowflakes drift,
A gentle touch, nature's gift.

Branches bow under weight so fine,
Nature's artistry, a design,
In hushed tones, the world is swayed,
With every flake, a promise made.

Silence reigns in the frozen air,
An ancient peace, beyond compare,
As twilight paints the world in gray,
Whispers of night lead dreams astray.

With every breath, the cold wraps tight,
An embrace of stillness, pure delight,
Wrapped in layers of frost and dreams,
Caught in the dance of winter's schemes.

So let us pause, in this sacred space,
To find our solace, our gentle grace,
In the silence of winter's breath,
Lies a beauty that conquers death.

The Breath of Winter's Embrace

In the hush of falling snow,
Whispers echo soft and low.
Frosted branches gently sway,
Nature wraps in white, at play.

Breezes chill the evening air,
Silent moments, dreams laid bare.
Stars peek through the winter's veil,
Tales of warmth in cold winds sail.

Crystals dance upon the ground,
In this stillness, peace is found.
Heartbeats slow with every sigh,
In winter's arms, we gently lie.

Footprints trace a path so pure,
Memories of days obscure.
In the night's embrace, we linger,
As warmth ignites with every finger.

A world wrapped tight in ice and snow,
A magic only winter knows.
We find solace in the chill,
As winter's breath brings quiet thrill.

A Journey Through the Frosted Dusk

When shadows stretch across the plains,
And daylight slowly wanes in chains.
The air turns crisp, a biting bite,
A journey starts into the night.

Frosted grass beneath our feet,
Echoes of the day retreat.
In twilight's glow, the world transforms,
As night awakens, magic swarms.

With every step, the silence reads,
A tale of nature's dormant seeds.
The moon begins its watchful rise,
While stars twinkle in the skies.

The calmness wraps like velvet deep,
As all the earth begins to sleep.
In stillness, find the beauty's grace,
A journey taken, heart's embrace.

The frosted dusk, a fleeting dream,
Softly glimmers, like a stream.
Through shadows deep, our spirits soar,
Together finding evermore.

Serenade of the Glacial Rivers

Where icy waters twist and flow,
A serenade of ebb and glow.
Every ripple sings a tune,
Softly under the watching moon.

The glaciers hum a timeless sound,
A melody through valleys found.
Gentle whispers in the breeze,
Carry stories with such ease.

Amongst the stones, the waters play,
In harmony, they laugh and sway.
Each moment holds a sweet refrain,
In nature's chorus, life's domain.

Reflections dance upon the stream,
A world alive, like waking dream.
With every curve, the rivers tease,
While shadows play between the trees.

Through valleys wide and canyons deep,
The glacial rivers softly creep.
Their serenade, a lasting hymn,
In frozen dawns, our spirits swim.

Luminescent Hues of Twilight

As daylight fades to pastel hues,
The world ignites with subtle cues.
Twilight paints in shades divine,
A canvas where our dreams align.

Crimson skies and golden beams,
We drift softly into dreams.
Shadows stretch and dance with grace,
In twilight's glow, we find our place.

The air is filled with whispered sighs,
As night unveils its velvet guise.
Stars ignite in twinkling dance,
A wondrous, fleeting, timeless chance.

The horizon glows with tender light,
Beneath the moon's enchanting sight.
In every color, peace reflects,
Our hopes and fears, the heart connects.

With every breath, we meet the dusk,
In twilight's arms, a sacred trust.
We weave our dreams and watch them soar,
In luminescent hues, explore.

Reverberations of Blue-tinged Skies

In the morning glow, whispers arise,
Clouds drift lightly, painted in sighs.
Birds take flight, their songs entwined,
A ballet of freedom, the sky's design.

Waves of azure stretch far and wide,
Where dreams take root, where hopes abide.
The sun descends, a fiery embrace,
Leaving behind its warm, golden trace.

Moments linger in twilight's embrace,
As shadows dance in this sacred space.
Reflections shimmer on the lake's face,
Time stands still in nature's grace.

Stars awaken, a tapestry spun,
Each one a story, the night begun.
Moonlight bathes the earth in peace,
In this quiet hour, all worries cease.

In reverberations of blue-tinged skies,
Life unfolds as the daylight flies.
We find our place in the vast divine,
In this stillness, our hearts align.

Timeless Dance of the Northern Lights

In the still of night, colors collide,
A waltz of hues, where dreams abide.
Emerald streaks in the velvet sky,
Whispers of magic, a cosmic sigh.

Lightning swirls in the frosty air,
A celestial ballet, beyond compare.
Each flicker tells tales of old,
Secrets of ages in brilliance bold.

As shadows play on the icy ground,
Elders of night, silent and profound.
We watch in awe as the world ignites,
Enveloped in wonder, hearts take flight.

Fleeting moments, yet timeless they seem,
Caught in the fabric of night's soft dream.
Nature's canvas reveals her grace,
The northern lights in a cosmic embrace.

In every ripple, history flows,
In sparkling skies, the universe glows.
Timeless dance, ever so bright,
Guiding lost souls through the night.

Songs of the Starlit Treetops

Beneath the arch of the endless night,
Whispers of leaves weave soft delight.
Treetops glisten with starlit dreams,
Nature's own choir, in harmony beams.

The wind carries tales, both old and new,
Each note a treasure, a world to pursue.
Rustling branches create a sweet sound,
A melody lost, yet found all around.

As crickets hum their gentle refrain,
The night deepens, knitting joy and pain.
Stars twinkle brightly, a celestial fit,
Illuminating paths where shadows sit.

Moonbeams cascade, soft silken threads,
Weaving through branches, where magic spreads.
In the heart of the woods, silence sings,
Life's hidden wonders, boundless offerings.

Songs of the starlit treetops soar,
Echoing dreams we cannot ignore.
In the quiet hush of the vibrant night,
We find our peace, a pure delight.

Embracing Solitude in the White Wilderness

Amidst the snow, vast and serene,
Where silence reigns, and peace is seen.
Footprints mark the untouched ground,
In solitude's arms, tranquility found.

Frigid winds whisper through bare trees,
Nature's breath carried with ease.
A world enshrouded, pure and bright,
In winter's embrace, heart takes flight.

Mountains rise like guardians tall,
In their shadows, we heed the call.
Each snowflake falls, a delicate art,
Painting the landscape, touching the heart.

As twilight glows, stars make their claim,
In the open expanse, we are the same.
Embracing the stillness, letting it guide,
In white wilderness, soul bared with pride.

A journey within in the frozen domain,
Finding our strength, our joy, our pain.
In solitude's warmth, we softly dive,
In nature's vastness, we feel alive.

Serenade of the Snow-laden Branches

In twilight's hush, the branches bow,
With heavy coats of soft white snow.
They whisper tales of winters past,
While moonlight dances, shadows cast.

The winds sing low, a gentle tune,
As stars emerge, bright as a boon.
Each flake that falls, a story spun,
In silence soft, the night's begun.

Beneath the boughs, the world seems still,
A moment caught, a heart to fill.
The frost-kissed air wraps tight around,
In nature's grace, pure peace is found.

As dawn approaches, colors bloom,
The icy veil begins to loom.
But in the night, the magic stays,
A serenade in frosty ways.

Where once was cold, now warmth's embrace,
Yet memories of winter's grace.
Forever held in tender light,
The snow-laden branches glow so bright.

Windswept Dreams of Distant Mountains

Beyond the peaks where eagles soar,
The dreams of ages whisper more.
With every gust, the valleys sigh,
Beneath the vast and open sky.

The trails unknown, they beckon near,
Each step a song, a note sincere.
With every breath, the world unfolds,
A tale of wanderers, brave and bold.

Through rocky crags and fields of gold,
The heart of nature's nestled hold.
In every breeze, a secret's cast,
From future to the echoing past.

As shadows dance on rivers wide,
In dreams of mountains, hope will ride.
With each ascent, the spirit gleams,
On windswept trails, we chase our dreams.

In twilight's glow, the world stands still,
A journey penned by fate and will.
Awash in hues of dusk's embrace,
We find ourselves, we find our place.

Melodies of the Midnight Sun

When daylight fades in vibrant hues,
The sun takes flight, a winding muse.
In sterile light, the shadows blend,
As night and gold begin to mend.

The echoes twine in dance and swirl,
With every note, the soft rays twirl.
A lullaby from skies above,
In every pulse, a thread of love.

The world awakes to twilight's call,
In precious moments, we stand tall.
With arms outstretched to skies aglow,
We sing along to the golden show.

In fleeting hours, where dreams reside,
The magic swells, a timeless tide.
With every heartbeat, memories spun,
The sweetest serenade of sun.

At dawn's soft kiss, the day will blend,
Yet in our souls, these melodies send.
A cadence born of light and night,
Forever cherished, pure delight.

The Stillness of Eternal Frost

When every breath holds winter's sigh,
The stillness glows, a knowing eye.
With icy fingers, time is traced,
In silent realms, our hearts embraced.

The world adorned in crystal sheen,
Each breath a cloud, so soft, serene.
In this embrace, the moments wait,
For whispers bold from nature's gate.

The trees stand tall, adorned in white,
Guardians of dreams in endless night.
In frozen stillness, longing stirs,
While peace descends, and silence purrs.

As shadows creep and twilight calls,
The frozen landscape gently sprawls.
With open hearts, we find our way,
In stillness, life begins to play.

In every flake that hits the ground,
Eternal peace is swiftly found.
For in this frost, we learn to see,
The beauty lies in simply being free.

Silhouettes of Frosted Pines

Silhouettes against the moon,
Embroidered in silver light,
Whispers dance with winter's tune,
As shadows grace the silent night.

Branches draped in icy lace,
Crisp breaths paint the frosty air,
Nature's still and tranquil space,
Holds secrets hidden, rare.

Cloaked in white, the pines stand tall,
Guardians of a world so pure,
Their quiet strength will never fall,
In silent watch, they shall endure.

Beneath the stars, they sway and bend,
Carved by winds both fierce and kind,
In the twilight, echoes blend,
Nature's solace, peace we find.

In this realm of frozen dreams,
Where time drifts like a feather light,
Frosted whispers stir in streams,
As nature breathes through the night.

Echoes Beneath the Aurora

Colors dance across the sky,
Whispers of the night unfold,
Beneath the dreamlike canvas high,
Ancient tales in hues retold.

Winds carry notes of ages past,
Songs of glimmers, sparks of fire,
Underneath the canopy vast,
Hearts ignite with pure desire.

Each flicker tells a story bright,
Of lovers lost and worlds reborn,
In the depths of the shimmering night,
The aurora's secrets beckon, worn.

Snowflakes fall like gentle sighs,
Their descent a silent prayer,
Echoes fill the frost-kissed skies,
A melody we all can share.

In this moment, time stands still,
Caught within a magic spell,
Awash in beauty, hearts we thrill,
Beneath the aurora, we dwell.

Call of the Snowy Vale

In the vale where silence reigns,
Snowflakes whisper on the ground,
Chill descends as moonlight wanes,
Echoes of the night resound.

Footprints lead to valleys deep,
Where dreams and shadows intertwine,
Nature holds her secrets steep,
Within the slopes, beneath the pine.

A haunting call of distant owls,
Lingers softly in the night,
Through the stillness, nature prowls,
Wrapped in silver, soft and white.

Starlit paths reveal their grace,
As frost ignites a cold embrace,
With every bend, a hidden space,
In snowy realms, we find our place.

Beneath the canopy of light,
Our hearts can wander, dare to roam,
In the snowy vale, so bright,
We'll carve our stories, make them home.

Secrets of the Icy Depths

In oceans deep where darkness sleeps,
Icy realms hold tales untold,
Whispers drift where silence keeps,
Secrets swathed in endless cold.

Glaciers guard their pristine grace,
Fractured beauty, crystal spun,
Beneath the waves, a hidden space,
Where time and light cannot outrun.

Starlit shimmers on the tide,
Unseen forces ebb and flow,
In the depths, where dreams abide,
The heart of winter's breath we know.

Echoes of the ancients call,
Bubbles rise like whispered lore,
In the icy depths, we enthrall,
Life in stillness, evermore.

From shadows deep, new worlds arise,
In frozen realms, we seek and yearn,
For every heart can find its prize,
In secrets of the icy churn.

Resilience of Tundra Spirits

In frozen whispers, secrets weave,
The tundra breathes, and spirits cleave.
With strength anew, they rise and soar,
Against the cold, they yearn for more.

Through icy winds, their voices call,
In silent nights, they stand so tall.
Embers glow in the darkest freeze,
Resilience flows in each crisp breeze.

Beneath the stars, the stories hum,
The heartbeats echo, they never succumb.
Through blizzards fierce and frosts that bite,
The tundra spirits embrace the night.

With snow-kissed dreams, they carve their way,
In shadows deep where the ancients play.
Their essence lingers, strong and bright,
Guiding lost souls through endless night.

In every flake, a tale unfolds,
Of strength in silence, of courage bold.
The tundra's heart beats ever strong,
In the dance of life, they belong.

Chronicles of the Midnight Realm

Beneath the moon's soft, silver glow,
A midnight realm where shadows flow.
Whispers twine in the velvet air,
Secrets hidden, treasures rare.

The starlit paths invite the brave,
To seek the truths the night can pave.
In quiet glades where dreams take flight,
The chronicles weave through endless night.

Echoes of laughter, sighs of pain,
In the midnight dance, joy and disdain.
Every heartbeat marks the space,
Of fleeting moments and timeless grace.

Ghostly figures waltz through trees,
Crafting legends on twilight's breeze.
Through twilight's cloak, they'll wonder far,
Beneath the watchful eyes of stars.

Each glance reveals a tale untold,
In shadows deep, where bravery's bold.
Chronicles bound in whispered dreams,
The midnight realm, where magic gleams.

Fables of the Celestial Wilderness

In valleys deep where legends stand,
Celestial fables paint the land.
With constellations as their guides,
They traverse fate, where hope abides.

The mountains echo ancient songs,
Of mighty roots and where heart belongs.
Each breeze carries a story bright,
In the celestial wilderness, they ignite.

Through labyrinth trails where spirits roam,
Adventures call, they find their home.
With every star, a path they trace,
In nature's arms, they find their grace.

Whispers of ages softly glimmer,
In twilight hues, hopes won't dimmer.
Fables born from the earth's embrace,
Celestial wonders, time can't erase.

In twilight's glow, the creatures meet,
With hearts as wild as each heartbeat.
Fables told in a language clear,
In the wilderness, no bounds appear.

Frostbitten Memories of Yesteryears

Upon the frost, memories lie,
Whispers of warmth, time passing by.
Each layer thick with stories told,
Frostbitten dreams of days of old.

The chill of winter, a bittersweet hue,
Recalling laughter, the moments few.
In ice and snow, our trails remain,
Echoes of joy, or echoes of pain.

With every flake, nostalgia swirls,
A dance of time where memory unfurls.
Bittersweet, the silence sings,
Of childhood games and fleeting springs.

Through crystal nights, reflections gleam,
In frosty breaths, we chase the dream.
Frostbitten tales of love and loss,
Carved in time, no matter the cost.

In twilight's grasp, the past appears,
We treasure softly our frostbitten years.
Embracing memories, we find our way,
Through chilly nights and the dawn of day.

Portraits of Glimmering Snowflakes

Each flake unique in silent dance,
A twirl of crystal, a fleeting chance.
Beneath the light, they sparkle bright,
In winter's embrace, a pure delight.

Glistening softly on the ground,
Nature's art, so profoundly found.
With every gust, they drift and sway,
Whispering secrets of winter's play.

They twinkle under the silver moon,
Holding magic that ends too soon.
A fleeting moment, so divine,
In the chill, they intertwine.

In awe, we watch them flutter down,
A beautiful cloak for the sleeping town.
Each one a dream, a wish, a sigh,
In the hush of night, they softly lie.

Portraits made of icy lace,
Nature's gift, a cold embrace.
In their glimmer, stories unfold,
Of winter's heart, a sight to behold.

Night Whispers in Frosted Fields

Under the stars, the silence speaks,
In frosted fields, the stillness creeps.
Moonlight bathes the world in glow,
Where dreams and shadows gently flow.

The grass a blanket, crisp and cold,
Each whisper tells a tale untold.
With every breath, the night awakes,
A symphony of sighs it makes.

Glimmers dance on frosty blades,
Nature's secrets in silent shades.
A soft rustle, the breeze takes flight,
In the depths of this quiet night.

Stars above like diamonds shine,
Guiding spirits through the pine.
As shadows lengthen, hearts ignite,
In the embrace of luminous night.

Whispers weave through trees and grass,
Carried by winds as moments pass.
In frosted fields, in dreams we find,
A sacred treasure in the mind.

Odes to the Celestial Aurora

Colors cascade across the sky,
A dance of light where dreams can fly.
Green, red, and gold in vibrant hues,
Painting the night with the heavens' muse.

Whispers of cosmic tales untold,
A canvas wide, a shimmer bold.
Each pulse a heartbeat, the universe sings,
As magic unfolds on celestial wings.

Beneath the glow, we stand in awe,
Transfixed by beauty, we barely draw breath.
Nature's wonder as night does sweep,
In the tapestry of starry deep.

With every arc, the sky ignites,
Capturing hearts under starlight nights.
A fleeting memory, a kiss divine,
In the heart of the night, the world aligns.

Oden to the aurora, a gift from above,
Enchanting souls with its radiant love.
In the stillness, we find our grace,
Chasing the light in the endless space.

Shadows of the Moonlit Vale

In the vale where shadows play,
Beneath the moon's soft, silver ray.
Whispers linger in the air,
Carrying secrets, light as a prayer.

Trees stand tall, their branches bare,
Guardians of dreams, in the chill they share.
The night wraps gently around the glade,
Where fantasies bloom and fears do fade.

Twinkling stars like jewels adorn,
The vast expanse, the night reborn.
In the stillness, a world unfolds,
Of stories lurking, waiting to be told.

Tread softly where the shadows roam,
In the vale, you may find home.
The flicker of hope in a gentle breeze,
Bringing solace with autumn leaves.

Cloaked in twilight, dreams take flight,
Each moment captured in the night.
With inky skies and a heart so free,
We wander deep, where all can be.

The Heartbeat of the North Wind

In the chill where whispers play,
The north wind sings a ghostly tune,
Through frozen trees, it weaves its way,
A melody beneath the moon.

Each gust a story, old and wise,
Of ancient tales that time forgot,
It carries secrets in the skies,
A breath of frost, a breath of thought.

With every shiver, life awakes,
The heartbeat thunders, yet it's calm,
The earth beneath, it gently shakes,
Caressed by nature's soothing balm.

From mountain peaks to valleys low,
The north wind moves, both fierce and kind,
A dance of ice and drifting snow,
In every echo, love you'll find.

As night descends, the shadows play,
In twilight's hold, it swirls and bends,
The north wind whispers come what may,
A timeless song that never ends.

Glacial Echoes of Forgotten Times

Beneath the weight of endless ice,
A world preserved in crystal dreams,
Where silence holds its precious price,
And nature's hymn softly beams.

The glaciers whisper tales of yore,
Of mountains formed and rivers lost,
Each crack a voice, a distant roar,
They carry history's deep frost.

In twilight's glow, the shadows shift,
As ancient winds begin to sigh,
Each echo speaks of nature's gift,
In frozen realms, time passes by.

The stars above begin to dance,
Reflecting on the icy ground,
In glacial light, we take our chance,
In hidden depths, the past is found.

From ages gone, the echoes flow,
In every flake, a universe,
Through frigid realms where secrets grow,
The frozen tales we now traverse.

Tales of the Winter Moon

Beneath the gaze of winter's moon,
Soft shadows stretch across the land,
They whisper secrets of the night,
In silver light, they gently stand.

Each flake that falls has much to say,
A story woven in its flight,
From ancient woods to frozen bay,
They write their lore in purest white.

The lullabies of frostbite air,
Wrap hearths in warmth, a soft embrace,
While winter winds, with frosty flair,
Invite us close to nature's grace.

Under the moon, we dream and yearn,
As stars align and time stands still,
In every heart, a fire burns,
Awakening our deeper will.

So let us share the stories spun,
In dreams awakened by the cold,
The winter moon, our guiding sun,
In every tale, a truth unfolds.

Celestial Paintings on a Black Canvas

In the night where silence reigns,
Stars emerge, a vibrant sweep,
A canvas dark where beauty trains,
In cosmic tides, our spirits leap.

With every twinkle, dreams take flight,
A tapestry of fate and chance,
The galaxies begin their dance,
In endless realms of starry light.

Nebulas burst in colors bold,
Creating worlds with hues divine,
Each brushstroke whispers tales untold,
Of distant lands, and worlds that shine.

Time spirals in celestial spins,
As cosmos spins its endless tale,
In the vastness, hope begins,
A starlit path, we learn to sail.

So gaze upon this midnight show,
Let visions stir within your mind,
In every star, a chance to grow,
Celestial art, a dream defined.

Whispers of the Arctic Dawn

Softly glows the morning light,
Over fields of purest white.
Whispers ride the frosty air,
Nature's secrets, calm and rare.

The horizon blushes bright,
As stars fade from the night.
A symphony of frozen breeze,
Embraces all with gentle ease.

Silent shadows dance around,
Awakening the sleeping ground.
Footprints trace a tale untold,
Of frigid dreams, in silence bold.

The sun ascends, a fiery throne,
Warming hearts of ice and stone.
With every ray, the whispers sing,
Of new beginnings, hope they bring.

In this world of white and blue,
Every moment feels so new.
Whispers of the arctic air,
Fill the heart with gentle care.

Fragments of Frosted Memories

Memories drift like falling snow,
Each one a tale, soft and slow.
Frosted edges, crisp and bright,
Reflecting echoes of the night.

Buried deep beneath the chill,
Are stories time cannot still.
Each flake a whisper from the past,
Fragile spells that hold us fast.

A childhood laughter fills the air,
Moments frozen, light as air.
Trees adorned in crystal lace,
Carry the joy of a smiling face.

Through the haze of silver dreams,
Life unfolds in gentle streams.
Fragments of days like shards of glass,
Shimmering long after they pass.

Beneath the quilt of winter's night,
The heart remembers, pure delight.
Frosted memories, sweet and rare,
Carried softly on chilly air.

Ballad of the Northern Pines

Whispers rise among the trees,
Softly swaying with the breeze.
Northern pines stand proud and tall,
Guardians of the forest's call.

In their shadows, stories blend,
Nature's tunes that never end.
Roots entwined in sacred ground,
In their silence, wisdom found.

Beneath the stars, their branches sway,
Dancing gently, night and day.
Echoes of a timeless vow,
Nature's strength they wear somehow.

Seasons change, yet still they stand,
A stalwart watch o'er the land.
Ballad sung through wind and rain,
In their presence, we remain.

With every storm, they'll rise again,
Rooted deep through joy and pain.
Northern pines will always sing,
A hymn of life, forever spring.

Aurora's Lament in Silver Skies

Draped in hues of emerald light,
The sky awakens, dances bright.
Auroras weave their tale of woe,
In silver skies, their sorrows flow.

Flickering shadows paint the night,
Whispers of stars, lost from sight.
Celestial voices call and plead,
A lament born from cosmic need.

Each shimmer tells of dreams undone,
Of twilight tales, of battles won.
Colors clash, then gently fade,
Mysteries in the silence laid.

In this lull of nature's plight,
The heartbeats echo pure delight.
Aurora's dance, a fleeting sigh,
Reminding us to dream and fly.

As night surrenders to the dawn,
The silver skies whisper on.
In every hue, in every plight,
Aurora sings of love, of light.